Tarik O'Regan

MAGNIFICAT & NUNC DIMITTIS
Variations for Choir

NOVELLO

Magnificat & Nunc Dimittis

Notes on Performance

The *ripieno* choir forms the main corpus of singers and, although divisi throughout, requires at least two or three performers to a part. The *concertante* choir should be grouped separately, visibly so, as a quartet of singers (one to a part), or, at most, an octet (two to a part) if there are sufficient forces. Similarly, the instrumental soloist should be visibly separated from the *ripieno* choir, but not grouped with the *concertante* choir. The work is written without any amplification in mind; however, should circumstances demand, amplification of the instrumental soloist and/or the *concertante* choir might be deemed suitable.

Programme Note

The *Magnificat* and *Nunc Dimittis* were both commissioned, separately, by Timothy Brown for the Choir of Clare College, Cambridge. The former was premièred at the 2000 Spitalfields Winter Festival in London, while the latter was composed for a BBC broadcast in 2001.

Both are large-scale settings, designed to stand as concert works in their own right or to be paired together for liturgical purposes at Evensong. In each movement I have tried to recreate the Renaissance practice of alternating chant and polyphony from a contemporary perspective. The work is scored for double-choir; soprano, alto, tenor and bass soloists and a solo soprano saxophone or violoncello.

Tarik O'Regan
New York, November 2004

Duration

Magnificat: c. 8 minutes
Nunc Dimittis: c. 5 minutes

Parts

Solo soprano saxophone and violoncello parts are available on sale from the publisher.

Magnificat

in memoriam Christopher Rutter (17.v.1981–2.iii.2001)

Tarik O'Regan

* Sing as plainchant throughout
** Parts available on sale

2. Et exsultavit, spiritus meus in Deo salutari meo.

2. Et exsultavit, spiritus meus in Deo salutari meo.

2. Et exsultavit, spiritus meus in Deo salutari meo.

2. Et exsultavit, spiritus meus in Deo salutari meo.

*These passages are to be repeated, as rapidly as possible, without clouding the pronunciation. Performers are to move between the pitches *randomly*, commencing the first syllable on the first pitch. A murmuring effect is desired; performers within the same part should not change pitch together, but at different times.

4

3. Qui - a respexit humilitatem an - cil - lae su - ae: ecce enim ex hoc beatam me dicent omnes ge - ne - ra - ti - o - nes.

★ or a group, soprano or alto

4. Qui - a fe - cit,

4. Qui - a fe - cit,

4. Qui - a fe - cit,

4. Qui - a

* or a group, tenor or bass

12

Steady ♩ = 108

51 (SOLO)

RIPIENO

T.1

T.2
6. Fe-cit po-ten - ti-am, in bra-chi-o su-o: dis - per - sit su-per-bos men - te cor - dis su - i,

B.1&2
6. Fe-cit po-ten - ti-am, in bra-chi-o su-o: dis - per - sit su-per-bos men - te cor - dis su - i,

Steady ♩ = 108

CONCERTANTE

S.
6. Fe - po - ten - ti -

A.
6. Fe - po - ten -

T.
6. Fe - cit po -

B.
6. Fe - cit

Steady ♩ = 108

S.Sax.
flz.

Vc.

****Accented notes in the *concertante* group indicate the contiguous pitches of the chant melody as it permeates all four parts.

* or a group, soprano or alto

18

* or a group, tenor or bass

* sing in the rhythm of speech, as if singing a psalm

Cambridge, October 2000

★ or a small group of altos

Nunc Dimittis

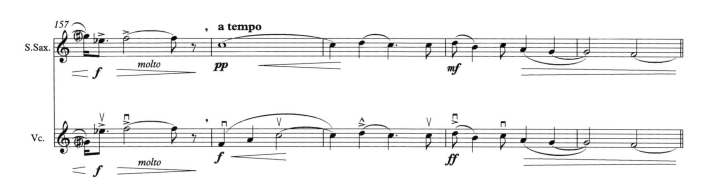

* sing as plainchant throughout

3. Quod pa - ra - sti ante faciem omnium po - pu - lo - rum:

* or a group, soprano or alto

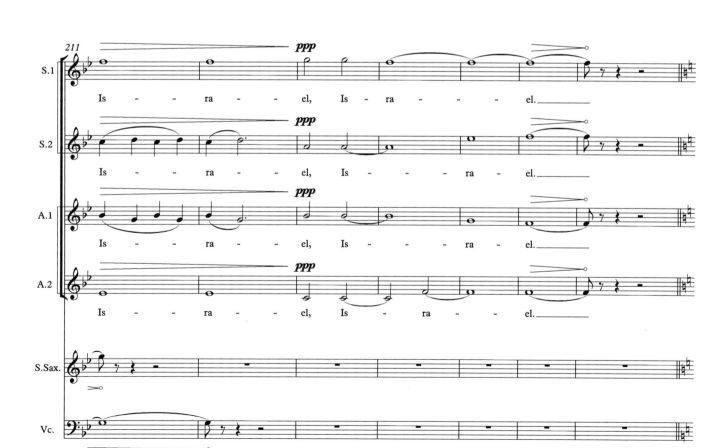

★ stagger breathing if necessary

Cambridge, February 2001

* or a group, soprano or alto

Texts: Latin

Magnificat

Canticle of the Blessed Virgin Mary (Luke I, vv. 46–55)

1. Magnificat anima mea Dominum.
2. Et exsultavit spiritus meus in Deo salutari meo.
3. Quia respexit humilitatem ancillae suae: ecce enim ex hoc beatam me dicent omnes generationes.
4. Quia fecit mihi magna qui potens est: et sanctum nomen eius.
5. Et misericordia eius a progenie in progenies timentibus eum.
6. Fecit potentiam in brachio suo: dispersit superbos mente cordis sui.
7. Deposuit potentes de sede, et exaltavit humiles.
8. Esurientes implevit bonis: et divites dimisit inanes.
9. Suscepit Israel puerum suum recordatus misericordiae suae.
10. Sicut locutus est ad patres nostros, Abraham et semini eius in saecula.
11. Gloria Patri, et Filio, et Spiritui Sancto.
12. Sicut erat in principio, et nunc, et semper, et in saecula saeculorum. Amen.

Nunc Dimittis

Song of Simeon (Luke II, vv. 29–32)

1. Nunc Dimittis servum tuum, Domine, secundum verbum tuum in pace.
2. Quia viderunt oculi mei salutare tuum.
3. Quod parasti ante faciem omnium populorum:
4. Lumen ad revelationem gentium, et gloriam plebis tuae Israel.
5. Glória Patri, et Fílio, et Spirítui Sancto.
6. Sicut erat in princípio, et nunc, et semper, et in sáecula saeculórum. Amen.

Texts: English

Magnificat

1. My soul doth magnify the Lord.
2. And my spirit hath rejoiced in God my Saviour.
3. For he hath regarded the lowliness of his hand-maiden: for, behold, from henceforth all generations shall call me blessed.
4. For he that is mighty hath magnified me: and holy is his name.
5. And his mercy is on them that fear him throughout all generations.
6. He hath showed strength with his arm: he hath scattered the proud in the imagination of their hearts.
7. He hath put down the mighty from their seat, and hath exalted the humble and meek.
8. He hath filled the hungry with good things: and the rich he hath sent empty away.
9. He remembering of his mercy hath holpen his servant Israel.
10. As he promised to our forefathers, Abraham and his seed, for ever.
11. Glory be to the father and to the Son, and to the Holy Ghost.
12. As it was in the beginning, is now, and ever shall be, world without end. Amen.

Nunc Dimittis

1. Lord, now lettest thou thy servant depart in peace, according to thy word.
2. For mine eyes have seen thy salvation.
3. Which thou hast prepared before the face of all people:
4. To be a light to lighten the Gentiles and to be the glory of thy people Israel.
5. Glory be to the father and to the Son, and to the Holy Ghost.
6. As it was in the beginning, is now, and ever shall be, world without end. Amen.

Order no. NOV200310
solo violoncello part NOV200310-01
solo soprano saxophone part
NOV200310-02

© 2004 Novello & Company Ltd.
Published in Great Britain by Novello
Publishing Limited

Exclusive Distributors:
Hal Leonard
7777 West Bluemound Road
Milwaukee, WI 53213
Email: info@halleonard.com

Hal Leonard Europe Limited
42 Wigmore Street
Marylebone, London, W1U 2RN
Email: info@halleonardeurope.com

Hal Leonard Australia Pty. Ltd.
4 Lentara Court
Cheltenham, Victoria, 3192 Australia
Email: info@halleonard.com.au

www.halleonard.com

Selected choral music by Tarik O'Regan

Alleluia, laus et gloria. Fanfare for SSA chorus
NOV200420

Bring rest, sweet dreaming child, for SATB chorus and harp
NOV050182; harp NOV050182-01

Corpus Christi Service, SATB and organ with congregation line
NOV200321

De Sancto Ioanne Baptista, for SATB chorus and organ
NOV954712

Dorchester Canticles, SATB chorus and organ NOV954701-01;
harp and percussion ad lib. NOV954701-02

Magnificat and Nunc Dimittis, for SATB chorus and solo soprano saxophone or violoncello
NOV200310; solo violoncello NOV200310-01; solo soprano saxophone NOV200310-02

Sequence for St Wulfstan:
Beatus auctor sæculi, for SATB chorus
NOV200277
O vera digna hostia, for SATB chorus
NOV200255
Tu claustra stirpe regia, for SATB chorus
NOV200266
Tu, Trinitatis Unitas, for SATB chorus
NOV200288

Threnody, for SATB chorus and strings
Vocal score NOV161205

NOVELLO